KNITTING BOOK

JOY GAMMON

Hippo Books
Scholastic Publications Limited
London

Scholastic Publications Ltd.,
10 Earlham Street, London WC2H 9RX, UK

Scholastic Inc.,
730 Broadway, New York, NY 10003, USA

Scholastic Canada Ltd.,
123 Newkirk Road, Richmond Hill,
Ontario L4C 3G5, Canada

Ashton Scholastic Pty Ltd.,
P O Box 579, Gosford, New South Wales,
Australia

Ashton Scholastic Ltd.,
165 Marua Road, Panmure, Auckland 6,
New Zealand

First published in the UK by Scholastic Publications Ltd., 1990
Copyright ©1990 Mirage Studios
Knitting pattern copyright © Joy Gammon 1990
Licensed by Copyright Promotions Ltd

ISBN 0 590 76514 0

Typeset by Christopher Smith Design, 4 Celbridge Mews, London
W2 6EU.

Made and printed in Spain by Mateu Cromo, S.A.

10 9 8 7 6 5 4 3 2 1

For further information on Wendy Yarns contact Wendy Wools,
Carter and Parker Limited, Gordon Mills, Guiseley, West
Yorkshire LS20 9PD.

Introduction

The four Teenage Mutant Hero Turtles have taken the world by storm. These unlikely pizza eating upholders of good against evil have captured everyone's imagination. Youngsters of all ages, and some not so young, want to wear jumpers with pictures of our fast talking friends on the front. So the idea for this book was born, and I'm sure you will want to knit up all the patterns.

There is a basic jumper pattern in the book, and you can choose to knit it with whichever of the pictures you like best on the front. Because the Turtles are very similar, except for the colour of their bandanas and the initial on their belts, you can knit any particular Turtle into any picture and the sleeves are cuffed and striped in a bandana colour too, echoing the elbow and wrist bands which the Turtles sport. The pictures include Raphael running, perhaps in hot pursuit of some baddie; Michaelangelo resting in the top of their sewer and smiling happily at the thought of his next pizza; Donatello standing proudly for his portrait and Leonardo cheering the Turtles' latest success. Way to go, guys.

The famous Turtle lettering is there, across the back of a jumper, and there is even a picture jumper of Splinter, all togged out in his pink. For a younger Turtle fan there is a pattern for a scarf with a portrait of each of our friends on it, and a hat with a rib which can be knitted in any of the bandana colours. Finally, for people who have a Turtle room, or would like the complete team of our Heroes on their settee, there is a set of cushions, four of course, each with one of the guys knitted into it.

So, let's rock and roll, dudes. Start knitting, and kit out all your Mutant Hero fans in the very latest in Turtle jumpers.

Cowabunga....

Joy Gammon

Teenage Mutant Hero Turtles Basic Jumper Pattern

SPECIAL NOTES

This is the basic pattern to be used to make five of the garments in this book, the four jumpers each with a different Turtle on the front, and the jumper with Splinter on the front. Splinter, the super-rat, is patterned here as a straightforward picture on the front of the basic pattern. The four Turtles are each knitted onto a jumper, each in a different pose, and each with his distinctive bandana and armband colour.

These colours and poses are:–

RAPHAEL running,
    bandana and stripe colour – red
MICHAELANGELO resting,
    bandana and stripe colour – orange
DONATELLO standing,
    bandana and stripe colour – purple
LEONARDO cheering,
    bandana and stripe colour – blue

Because the Turtles are otherwise so similar, any Turtle can be knitted in any of the poses simply by changing the bandana colour to that of the preferred Turtle and embroidering the appropriate initial in the centre of the belt buckle.

Each of the four jumpers with a Turtle on the front has the cuff ribs and a stripe in each sleeve also knitted in the bandana colour of the chosen Turtle.

For special instructions for these ribs and stripes, and also the materials for a specific jumper, see the individual notes for each pattern which accompany the chosen chart.

It would also be possible to knit the Turtle lettering from the chart on page 26 across the back of any of these jumpers, placing it as shown on the lettering chart.

Instructions are given for the smallest size first, with the the other sizes in brackets following or listed in order.

MEASUREMENTS

To fit sizes	26–28 66–71	30–32 76–81	34–36 86–91	38–40 in 97–102 cm
Actual size	30 76	35 89	39 99	43 in 109 cm
Length	20 51	22 56	23 58	24 in 61 cm
Under-arm	14 36	17 43	18 46	18 in 46 cm

MATERIALS

Refer to specific chosen pattern for yarn needed.

Also needed 1 pair 3¼mm (No 10) needles, 1 pair 4mm (No 8) needles

ABBREVIATIONS

K = Knit; P = Purl; st(s) = stitch(es); inc. = increase; dec. = decrease; beg. = beginning; cont. = continue; foll. = follow(ing); tbl. = through back of loop; rem. = remaining; st. st. = stocking stitch; tog. = together; patt. = pattern.

TENSION

24sts and 32 rows = 10cm (4in) in stocking stitch on 4mm (No. 8) needles.

FRONT

Using 3¼mm needles and main colour, cast on 87(99, 111, 123)sts. and work:-

Row 1 – K2, (P1, K1) to last st, K1.

Row 2 – K1, (P1, K1) to end.

Repeat these 2 rows until rib measures 5(5, 5, 6)cm ending with row 2, and inc by 4(6, 6, 6)sts evenly across this last row. (91, 105, 117, 129sts)

Change to 4mm needles and st. st. starting with a K row. **

Work the number of st. st. rows stated on the chosen chart in plain main colour before commencing chart.

With the next st. st. row as row 1 of the chart, commence to work from the chart placing it as shown.

Work straight until chart is complete then work the number of st. st. rows stated after the chart in plain main colour.

Shape neck:-

Cont in plain main colour, work the next row:-
K38(44, 49, 54) turn, leaving rem sts on a holder, P2 tog tbl, P to end.

*** Dec 1st. at neck edge only on next 2 rows, then on every alt row until 32(38, 43, 47)sts rem.

Work a further 10 (14, 14, 12) rows straight, so ending with a P row .

Cast off. ***

Rejoin yarn to inside edge of rem sts. K15(17, 19, 21)sts and place them on a holder, K to end .

Next row – P to last 2, P2 tog.
Rep from *** to ***.

BACK

Work as given for front as far as **.

Work straight in plain main colour until back matches front to shoulder, ending with a P row.

Next row – Cast off 32(38, 43, 47)sts, K until 32(38, 43, 47)sts rem, place the 27(29, 31, 35)sts just worked onto a holder, cast off to end.

SLEEVES

NB. If knitting one of the Turtle jumpers, note the special instructions on sleeves given for the chosen variation.

Using 3¼mm needles, cast on 43(47, 51, 55)sts and work 5(5, 5, 6)cm in rib in the same way as given for the front welt, ending with row 2 and inc by 1st. at end of this row. (44, 48, 52, 56sts)

Change to 4mm needles and st. st. and inc 1st. each end of the first, then every foll 4th row until there are 90(102, 108, 114)sts.

Cont straight to a total length of 36(43, 46, 46)cm ending with a P row.

Cast off loosely.

NECKBAND

In main colour throughout.

Press according to ball band instructions. Join left shoulder seam.

Using 3¼mm needles and with right side facing, pick up and K the 27(29, 31, 35)sts from the back neck holder working 2tog in the centre, 19(21, 21, 22)sts down the left neck slope, the 15(17, 19, 21)sts from the front neck holder and 19(21, 21, 22)sts up the right neck slope. (79, 87, 91, 99sts)

Starting with row 2, work 8(10, 10, 10) rows of rib in the same way as before so ending with a right side row, a row 1 of the rib.

K1 row.

Starting with row 1 of the rib, rib 8(10, 10, 10) further rows.

Cast off very loosely in rib.

TO MAKE UP

Join rem seams, ensuring that armholes are 19(22, 23, 24)cm deep after making up. Using the chart and picture as a guide, embroider detail.

Running Turtle Jumper - Raphael

MATERIALS

WENDY Family Choice Double Knitting in:

Main colour
    Black (247)   5 6 7   8 x 50gm balls
Bandana & Stripe colour
    Red (242)   1 1 1   1 x 50gm ball
    Green (932)   1 1 1   1 x 50gm ball

Small quantities of Dark Green (244), Yellow (903), White (212) and Grey (239)

VARIATIONS ON THE BASIC PATTERN

This jumper is knitted in black throughout, with the picture of Raphael running knitted on the front, placed as given on the chart. The sleeves are striped in the bandana colour to echo the wrist and elbow bands of the chosen Turtle. Work these stripes as follows:–
Cast on and work cuff rib in bandana colour. Commence st. st. in main colour and work sleeve as given to a total length from cast on edge of 14(18, 19, 19)cm.
Cont to shape sleeve as given, change to bandana colour and work 22(28, 30, 30) rows. Complete sleeve as given in main colour.

Key **All colour blocks as marked:**
G   = **Green**
DG   = **Dark Green**
R   = **Red**
Y   = **Yellow**
W   = **White**
Gr   = **Grey**
All rem. sts. main colour (Black)=B
– – – – Embroidery lines

After completing chart work a further
2(4, 6, 8) rows before neck shaping.

Centre ↓ Stitch

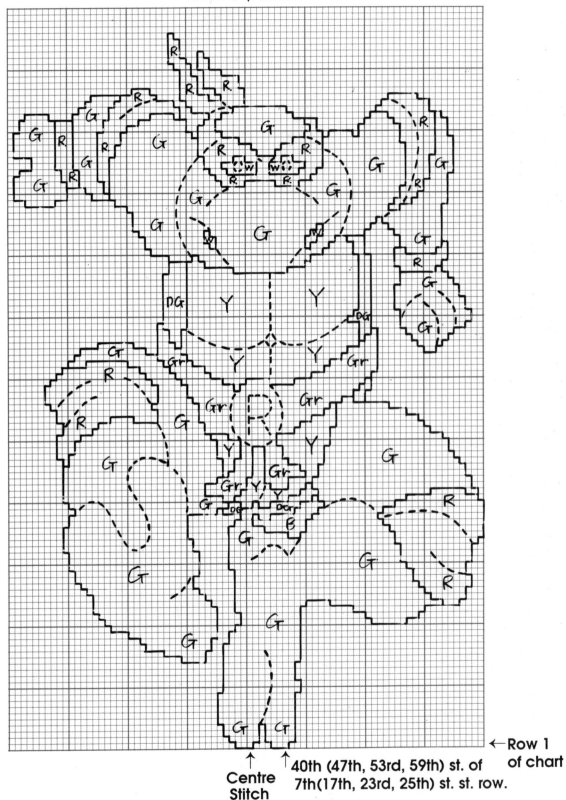

← Row 1
of chart

↑ Centre
Stitch

↑ 40th (47th, 53rd, 59th) st. of
7th(17th, 23rd, 25th) st. st. row.

Work 6(16, 22, 24) main colour st. st. rows before commencing chart.

9

Resting Turtle Jumper -Michaelangelo

MATERIALS

WENDY Family Choice Double Knitting in:

Main colour
  Red (242)   5 6 7 8 x 50gm balls
Bandana & Stripe colour
  Orange (197) 1 1 1 1 x 50gm ball

Small quantities of Green (932), Dark Green (244), Black (247), Pale Grey (239), White (212), Yellow (903) and Dark Grey (931).

VARIATIONS ON THE BASIC PATTER

This jumper is knitted in red throughout, with the picture of Michaelangelo resting knitted on the front, placed as given on the chart. The sleeves are striped in the bandana colour to echo the wrist and elbow bands of the chosen Turtle. Work these stripes as follows:–
Cast on and work cuff rib in bandana colour. Commence st. st. in main colour and work sleeve as given to a total length from cast on edge of 14(18, 19, 19)cm.
Cont to shape sleeve as given, change to bandana colour and work 22(28, 30, 30) rows. Complete sleeve as given in main colour.

Key All colour blocks as marked:
G   = Green
Y   = Yellow
DG   = Dark Green
O   = Orange
B   = Black
Gr   = Dark Grey
PG   = Pale Grey
W   = White
All rem. sts. main colour (Red)
– – – – Embroidery lines

RESTING TURTLE – MICHAELANGELO™
CHART FOR FRONT

Work a further 16(18, 18, 20) main colour st. st. rows after completion of chart before neck shaping.

Centre ↓ Stitch

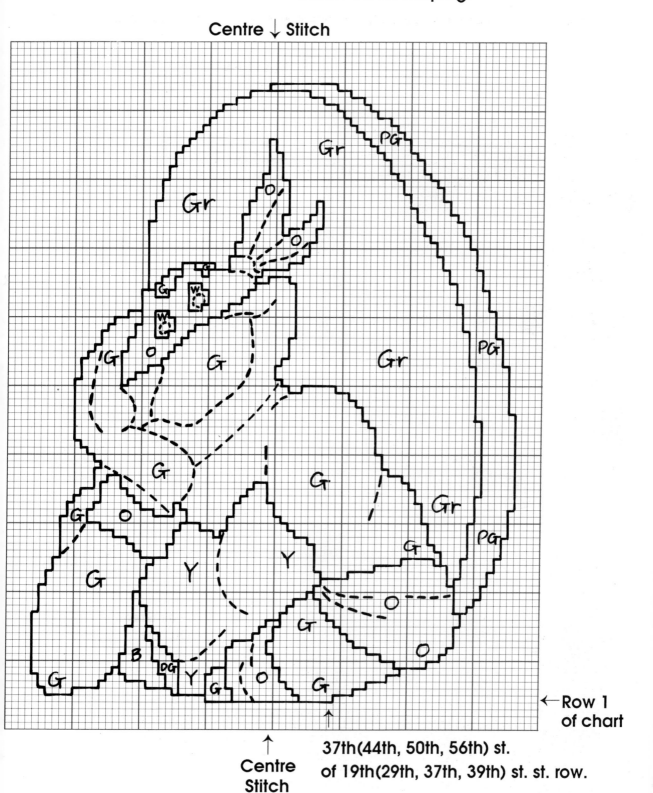

← Row 1 of chart

↑
Centre
Stitch

37th(44th, 50th, 56th) st.
of 19th(29th, 37th, 39th) st. st. row.

Work 18(28, 36, 38) main colour st. st. rows before chart.

13

Standing Turtle Jumper -Donatello

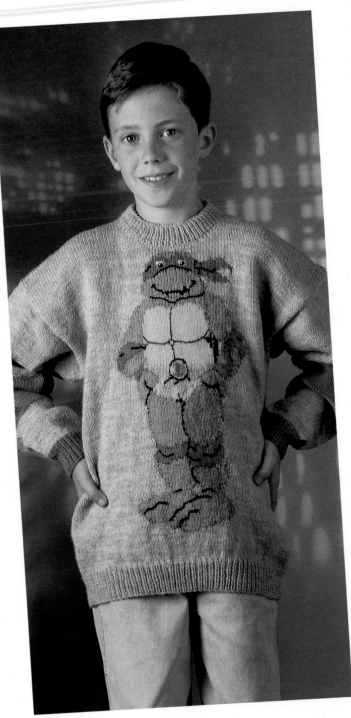

MATERIALS
WENDY Family Choice Double Knitting in:

Main colour
Grey (239)   5 6 7 8 x 50gm balls
Bandana & Stripe colour
Purple (249)   1 1 1 1 x 50gm ball
Green (932)   1 1 1 1 x 50gm ball

Small quantities of Dark Green (244), Pink (923), Yellow (903), Black (247) and White (212)

VARIATIONS ON THE BASIC PATTERN

This jumper is knitted in grey throughout, with the picture of Donatello standing knitted on the front, placed as given on the chart. The sleeves are striped in the bandana colour to echo the wrist and elbow bands of the chosen Turtle. Work these stripes as follows:–
Cast on and work cuff rib in bandana colour. Commence st. st. in main colour and work sleeve as given to a total length from cast on edge of 14(18, 19, 19)cm.
Cont to shape sleeve as given, change to bandana colour and work 22(28, 30, 30) rows. Complete sleeve as given in main colour.

Key **All colour blocks as marked:**
G   = **Green**
Y   = **Yellow**
P   = **Purple**
Gr   = **Grey**
DG   = **Dark Green**
B   = **Black**
Pi   = **Pink**
W   = **White**
All rem. sts. main colour (Grey)
– – – – Embroidery lines

STANDING TURTLE – DONATELLO™
CHART FOR FRONT

Work 2(4, 6, 8) further st. st. rows before
commencing neck shaping.

Centre ↓ Stitch

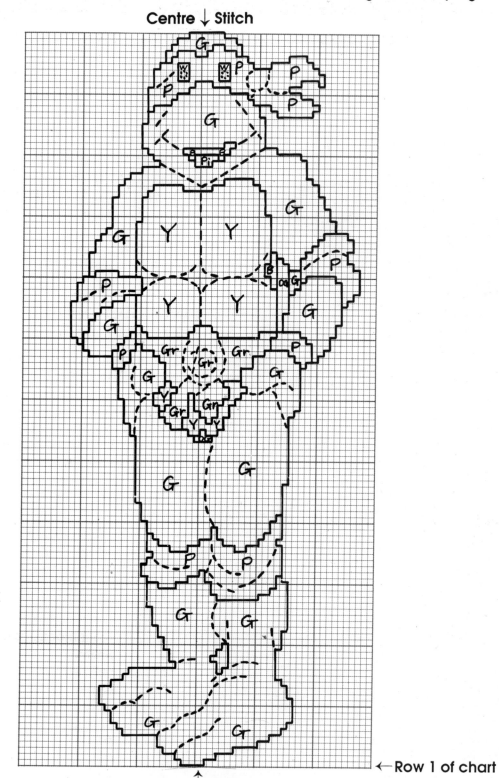

←Row 1 of chart

Centre ↑ Stitch
= 46th(53rd, 59th, 65th) st. of 3rd(13th, 19th, 21st) st.st. row.

Work 2(12, 18, 20) rows in st.st. in main colour before chart.

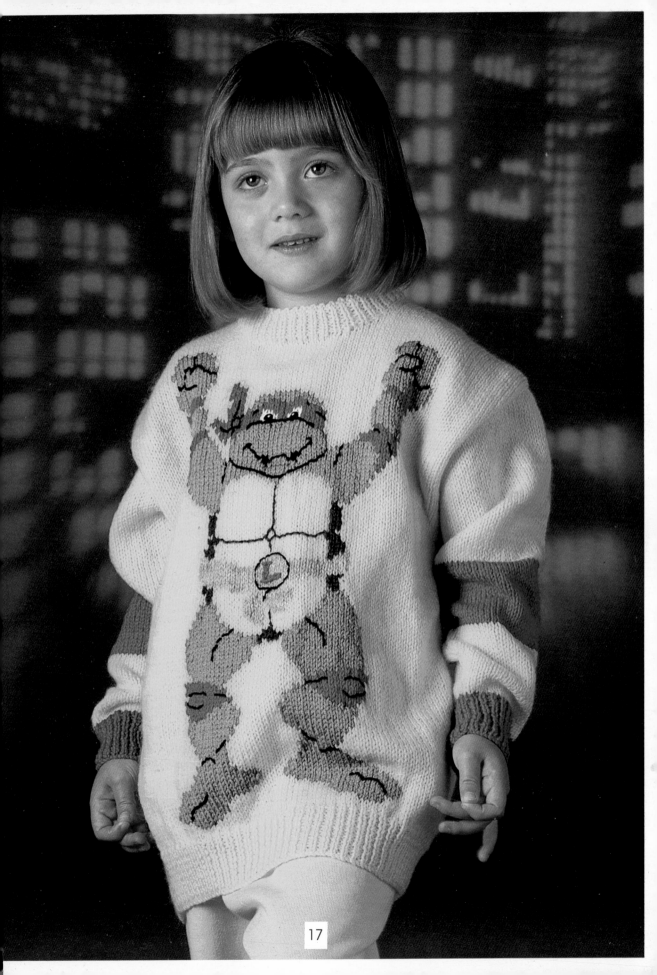

Cheering Turtle Jumper - Leonardo

MATERIALS

WENDY Family Choice Double Knitting in:

Main colour
   Yellow (903)   5   6   7   8 x 50gm balls
Bandana & Stripe colour
   Blue (206)   1   1   1   1 x 50gm ball
   Green (932)   1   1   1   1 x 50gm ball

Small quantities of Dark Green (244), White (212), Grey (239), Black (247) and Pink (923)

VARIATIONS ON THE BASIC PATTERN

This jumper is knitted in yellow throughout, with the picture of Leonardo cheering knitted on the front, placed as given on the chart. The sleeves are striped in the bandana colour to echo the wrist and elbow bands of the chosen Turtle. Work these stripes as follows:–
Cast on and work cuff rib in bandana colour. Commence st. st. in main colour and work sleeve as given to a total length from cast on edge of 14(18, 19, 19)cm.
Cont to shape sleeve as given, change to bandana colour and work 22(28, 30, 30) rows. Complete sleeve as given in main colour.

Key All colour blocks as marked:
G	=	Green
B	=	Blue
DG	=	Dark Green
Y	=	Yellow
Gr	=	Grey
Bl	=	Black
P	=	Pink
W	=	White

All rem. sts. main colour (Yellow)
– – – – Embroidery lines

Work 0(4,6,6) rows st. st. before neck shaping

Centre ↓ Stitch

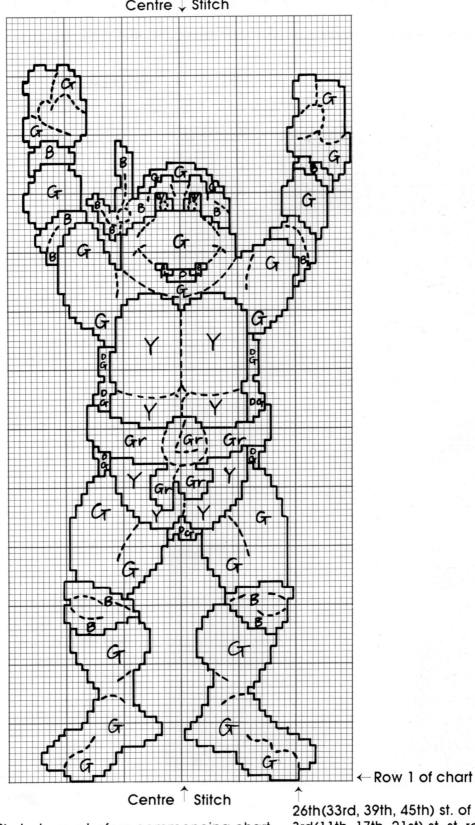

← Row 1 of chart

Centre ↑ Stitch

26th(33rd, 39th, 45th) st. of
3rd(11th, 17th, 21st) st. st. row

Work 2(10, 16, 20) st. st. rows before commencing chart.

Splinter Jumper

MATERIALS

WENDY Family Choice Double Knitting in:

Main colour
Royal Blue (217) 5   6   7   8 x 50gm balls

Part balls of Pink (199) and Brown (227)
Small quantities of Grey (931), White (212) and
Black (247)

VARIATIONS ON THE BASIC PATTERN

This jumper is knitted in royal blue throughout,
with the picture of Splinter knitted on the front,
placed as given on the chart. The sleeves are
plain main colour.

Key **All colour blocks as marked:**
B   = Brown
W   = White
G   = Grey
BL   = Black
P   = Pink
All rem. sts. main colour (Royal Blue)
– – – – Embroidery lines

Work a further 0(4, 6, 6) st. st. rows
before neck shaping.

Centre ↓ Stitch

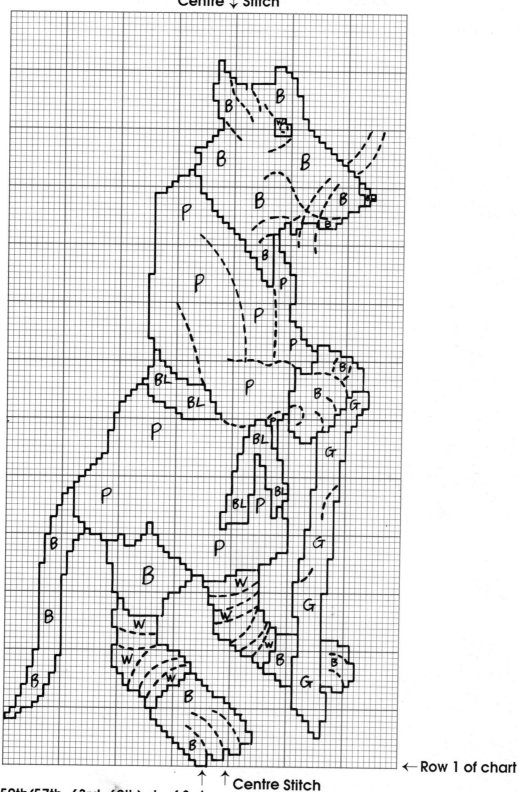

← Row 1 of chart

50th(57th, 63rd, 69th) st. of 3rd
(11th, 17th, 21st) st. st. row.

Centre Stitch

Work 2(10, 16, 20) main colour st. st. rows before
commencing chart.

Lettering Jumper

MATERIALS

WENDY Family Choice Double Knitting in:

Main colour

Navy (259)	5	6	7	8 x 50gm balls
Green (932)	1	1	1	1 x 50gm ball

MEASUREMENTS

To fit sizes	26–28 66–71	30–32 76–81	34–36 86–91	38–40 97–102	in cm
Actual size	30 76	35 89	39 99	43 109	in cm
Length	20 51	22 56	23 58	24 61	in cm
Under-arm	14 36	17 43	18 46	18 46	in cm

TENSION

24sts and 32 rows = 10cm (4in) in stocking stitch on 4mm (No. 8) needles.

BACK

Using 3¼mm needles and main colour, cast on 87(99, 111, 123)sts and work:–
Row 1 – K2, (P1, K1) to last st, K1.
Row 2 – K1, (P1, K1) to end.
Repeat these 2 rows until rib measures 5(5, 5, 6)cm ending with row 2, and inc by 4(6, 6, 6)sts evenly across this last row. (91, 105, 117, 129sts)
Change to 4mm needles and st. st. starting with a K row. **
Work straight to a total length of 38(42, 43, 44,)cm ending with a P row.
With the next st. st. row as row 1 of the chart, commence to work from the chart placing it as shown.
Work straight until chart is complete then work the number of st. st. rows stated after the chart in plain main colour.
Next row – Cast off 32(38, 43, 47)sts, K until 32(38, 43, 47)sts rem, place the 27(29, 31, 35)sts just worked onto a holder, cast off to end.

FRONT

Work as given for back as far as **.
Work straight in plain main colour until front is 20(24, 24, 24) rows shorter than the back, so ending with a P row.

Shape neck:–

Cont in plain main colour, work the next row:–
K38(44, 49, 54) turn, leaving rem sts on a holder, P2 tog tbl, P to end.
*** Dec 1st. at neck edge only on next 2 rows, then on every alt row until 32(38, 43, 47)sts rem.
Work a further 10(14, 14, 12) rows straight, so ending with a P row.
Cast off.***

25

Rejoin yarn to inside edge of rem sts. K15(17, 19, 21)sts and place them on a holder, K to end.
Next row – P to last 2, P2 tog.
Rep from *** to ***.

SLEEVES

Using 3¼mm needles, cast on 43(47, 51, 55)sts and work 5(5, 5, 6)cm in rib in the same way as given for the front welt, ending with row 2 and inc by 1st. at end of this row. (44, 48, 52, 56sts)
Change to 4mm needles and st. st. and inc 1st. each end of the first, then every foll 4th row until there are 90(102, 108, 114)sts.
Cont straight to a total length of 36(43, 46, 46)cm ending with a P row.
Cast off loosely.

NECKBAND

In main colour throughout.
Press according to ball band instructions. Join left shoulder seam.
Using 3¼mm needles and with right side facing, pick up and K the 27(29, 31, 35)sts from the back neck holder working 2tog in the centre, 19(21, 21, 22)sts down the left neck slope, the 15(17, 19, 21)sts from the front neck holder and 19(21, 21, 22)sts up the right neck slope. (79, 87, 91, 99sts)
Starting with row 2, work 8(10, 10, 10) rows of rib in the same way as before so ending with a right side row, a row 1 of the rib.
K1 row.
Starting with row 1 of the rib, rib 8(10, 10, 10) further rows.
Cast off very loosely in rib.

TO MAKE UP

Join rem seams, ensuring that armholes are 19(22, 23, 24)cm deep after making up. Using chart and picture as a guide, embroider detail.

> **Key**
> **All colour blocks labelled G = Green**
> **All rem. sts. main colour (Navy)**
> **– – – – Embroidery lines**

LETTERING JUMPER CHART FOR BACK

Work a further 14(18, 20, 24) rows to complete back.

Centre ↓ Stitch

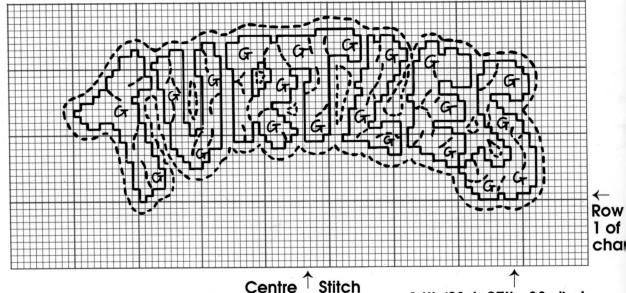

Centre ↑ Stitch

←Row 1 of chart

↑ 14th(21st, 27th, 33rd) st.

Turtle Hat & Scarf Set

MATERIALS

WENDY Family Choice Double Knitting in:

Main colour Yellow (903)   3 x 50gm balls

Part ball of Blue (206) (or any other bandana colour if preferred)
Small quantities of Green (932), Pink (923), Black (247), White (212), Purple (249), Orange (197) and Red (242).

1 pair 3¾mm (No. 9) and 1 pair 4mm (No. 8) needles.

MEASUREMENTS

The scarf is approximately 102cm (40in) long and the hat is approximately 36cm (14in) in diameter.

TENSION

24sts and 32 rows = 10cm (4in) in stocking stitch on 4mm (No. 8) needles.

HAT

Using 3¾mm needles and blue, cast on 107sts. and work:–
Row 1 – K2, (P1, K1) to last st, K1.
Row 2 – K1, (P1, K1) to end.
Repeat these 2 rows until rib measures 5cm ending with row 2 and inc by 1st. at end of this row. (108sts)
Change to 4mm needles, yellow and st. st. starting with a K row, and work 24 rows, so ending with a P row.
Next row – (K2 tog, K23, K2 tog tbl) 4 times. (100sts)
Next and every alt row – P.
Next K row – (K2 tog, K21, K2 tog tbl) 4 times. (92sts)
Next K row – (K2 tog, K19, K2 tog tbl) 4 times. (84sts)
Cont in this way, keeping decreasings above

one another, dec by 8sts on every K row and so working 2sts less between decreasings until 20sts rem. Run a thread through rem sts, pull tight and use to join back seam of yellow part of hat. Seam rib in blue.

SCARF

On 4mm needles throughout.
Cast on 61sts in yellow and work:–
Row 1 – K.
Row 2 – P15, K1, P29, K1, P rem 15.
Rep these 2 rows throughout rem of work so creating 2 vertical lines of rev sts where the sides of the scarf will fold; AT THE SAME TIME place the motifs:–
Work 4 rows in yellow.
* Commence motif on next row, working this as row 1 of motif and placing it as given.
Complete all 17 rows of motif with Bandana colour (B) as blue.
Work 3 further rows. *
Repeat from * to * but with Bandana colour as Orange.
Repeat from * to * but with Bandana colour as Purple.
Repeat from * to * but with Bandana colour as Red.
When all four motifs are complete, cont to repeat the 2 rows in yellow only until scarf measures 102cm, ending with row 2.
Cast off loosely.

TO MAKE UP

Press according to ball band instructions.
Make a 5cm diameter yellow pom-pom and attach to the top of the hat.
Using the chart and picture as a guide, embroider detail. Join the back seam of the scarf and fringe the ends in yellow.

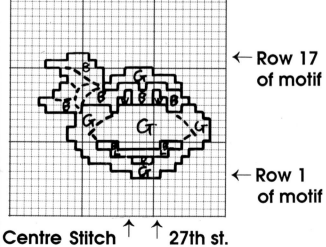

HAT & SCARF SET
MOTIF FOR SCARF

← Row 17 of motif

← Row 1 of motif

Centre Stitch ↑   ↑ 27th st.

Key All colour blocks as marked:		
G	=	Green
P	=	Pink
Bl	=	Black
W	=	White
B	=	Bandana colour (see pattern)

All rem. sts. main colour (Yellow)

– – – – Embroidery lines

Turtle Cushions

SPECIAL NOTE

The same picture is knitted here on each of four cushions. Using the same chart for each cushion, the bandana and armband colour is changed and the embroidered initial, so that each picture becomes one of the distinctive Turtles. The background colours are four subtly different neutrals.

MATERIALS

WENDY Family Choice Double Knitting in:

For each of the Cushions, 3 x 50gm balls of chosen main colour in either: Cream (230), or warm Beige (225), or cold Beige (200), or dark Beige (202)

Plus, for each cushion, small quantities of Green (932), Yellow (903), Dark Green (244), Grey (239), Black (247), Pink (923), White (212) and the chosen Bandana colour, ie. either Red (242), or Purple (249), or Blue (206) or Orange (197).

For each cushion a 41cm (16in) square cushion pad or equivalent filling.

MEASUREMENTS

The cushion will be approx. 41cm (16in) square.

TENSION

24sts and 32 rows = 10cm (4in) in stocking stitch on 4mm (No. 8) needles.
Chosen needles and st. st. are used throughout.

CUSHION FRONT

Using 4mm needles and main colour, cast on 96sts.
Begin to work from the chart with the first row as row 1 of the chart, placing it as shown.

Complete the chart, then cont in plain main colour until work is square.
Cast off loosely.

CUSHION BACK

In plain main colour throughout.
On 4mm needles, cast on 96sts.
Work straight until back matches front. ie. is square.
Cast off loosely.

TO MAKE UP

Press according to ball band instructions.
Using chart and picture as a guide embroider details.
Seam front and back together inserting cushion pad or filling.

Key All colour blocks as marked:

G	= Green
Y	= Yellow
DG	= Dark Green
Gr	= Grey
Bl	= Black
P	= Pink
W	= White
B	= Bandana colour (see pattern)

All rem. sts. main colour
– – – – Embroidery lines

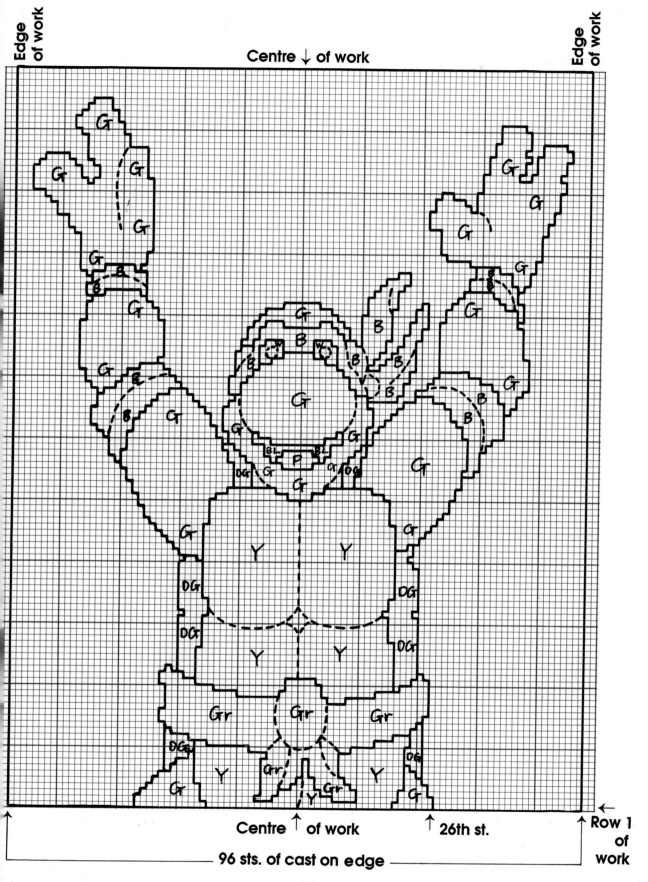